MACHINE TECHNOLOGY

Cutting Machines

Kay Davies and Wendy Oldfield

Titles in the series:

Cutting Machines

Digging Machines

Mixing Machines

Spinning Machines

Cover inset: This machine is cutting down, and collecting, wheat. It is called a combine harvester. Find out how the machine works on pages 24 – 5.

Title page: This man is using a chain saw to cut through a log. Find out more about chain saws on page 12.

Series and book editor: Geraldine Purcell
Series designer: Helen White
Series consultant: Barbara Shepherd, (former) LEA adviser on the Design and Technology National Curriculum.
Photo stylist: Zoë Hargreaves

First published in 1995 by Wayland (Publishers) Limited
61 Western Road, Hove, East Sussex BN3 1JD, England.

© Copyright 1995 Wayland (Publishers) Limited

British Library Cataloguing in Publication Data
Davies, Kay
 Cutting Machines. – (Machine Technology Series)
 I. Title II. Oldfield, Wendy III. Bull, Peter
 IV. Series
 621.93

ISBN 0 7502 1281 0

DTP design by White Design
Printed and bound by L.E.G.O. S.p.A., Vicenza, Italy.

Words in **bold** appear in the glossary on pages 30 – 31.

Contents

Cutting tools

Cutting blades are wedge, or V-shaped. They narrow to a sharpened edge. Cutting only takes place when a blade moves.

Knives use the **force** of a pull or a push to cut. When the blade is moved across an object the wedge forces the **material** out sideways. This cuts, or parts, the object. ▼

Cutting blades come in lots of shapes. Rotary cutters have circular blades. As the cutter is pushed, the blade turns and it cuts the material. ▼

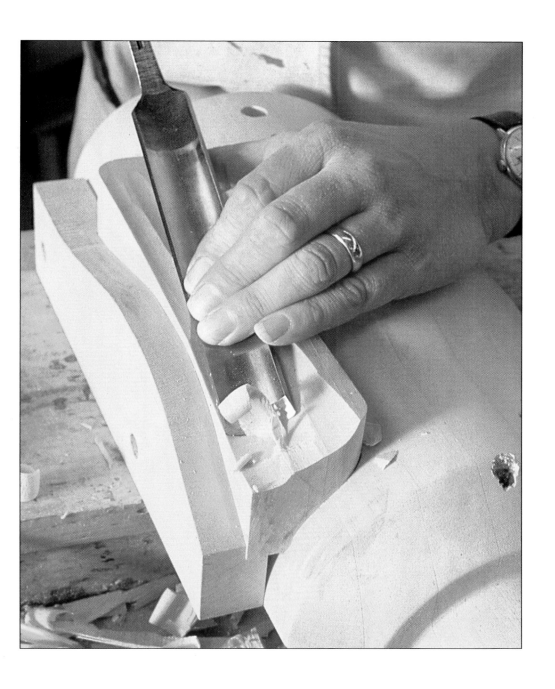

▲ Chisels are often used to shape wood. A chisel has a wedge-shaped blade on one side. The angled cutting blade uses a **bevel** action, which cuts the wood away from the person cutting the wood.

Cutting depth

Some cutting tools cut deeply and others remove only a thin layer from the surface of objects.

Vegetable peelers remove only the surface 'skin' from vegetables or fruit. The cutting edge is raised on a wide V–shaped blade. The cut skin curls neatly out of the way through a slot. ▼

▲ Wood planes are tools used by carpenters.
They are used to shave a thin slice from the
surface. This smoothes and shapes the wood.

The blade in a wood plane sticks out of a slit
in a smooth base. The blade can be moved
up and down to change the thickness of the
shavings.

Using scissors and pruners

▲ Scissors are much easier to use than knives for cutting cloth or paper.

There are two blades on scissors, which are sharpened into wedges. The blades are held together by a rod or screw which allows the blades to **pivot** so that both can move.

The blades act as **levers**. When they are brought together both cut from opposite directions, parting the material sideways. ▼

The action of scissors cutting

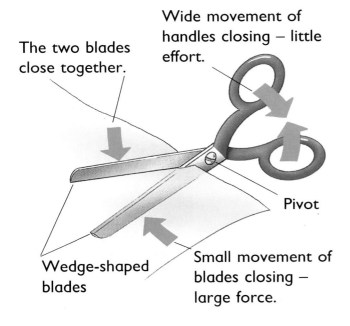

The two blades close together.

Wide movement of handles closing – little effort.

Pivot

Wedge-shaped blades

Small movement of blades closing – large force.

The action of pruners

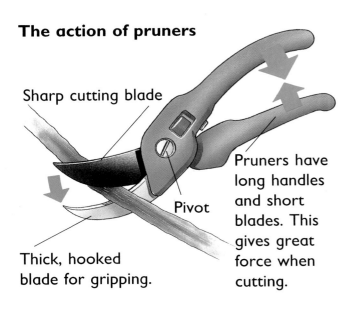

Sharp cutting blade

Pruners have long handles and short blades. This gives great force when cutting.

Pivot

Thick, hooked blade for gripping.

▲ Pruners are like scissors but are stronger. Pruners can be used for tough cutting jobs around the garden.

◀ Some pruners have hooked bottom blades which are used to grip twigs firmly. The upper blades are rounded so the two fit together when closed. The sharp upper blades cut the twigs.

9

Hand saws

Saws are long blades with many teeth. Each tooth has a cutting blade which faces forwards so the saw only cuts in one direction. The teeth stick out slightly to the right or the left. This makes a wide cut and stops the blade jamming in the wood. ▼

Action of saw cutting

Saws only cut when moved forward.

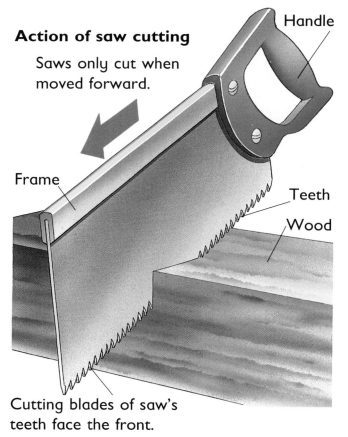

Handle

Frame

Teeth

Wood

Cutting blades of saw's teeth face the front.

▲ Bowsaws have a wide U-shaped frame. The blades are usually made from springy steel which can cut planks of wood or make shapes. Thicker blades can be fitted which can cut through logs.

▲ This boy is using a tenon saw which has a fine-toothed blade fixed to a strong, solid frame.

Mechanised saws

Saws driven by machines make cutting logs and tree trunks quick and easy.

Chain saws are usually driven by a small petrol **motor**. This turns a chain which is moved round a bar. The chain has cutting teeth shaped like small chisels round its edge. ▶

A chain saw in action

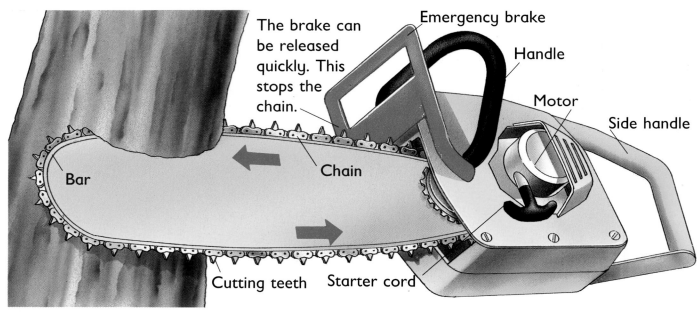

The brake can be released quickly. This stops the chain.

Emergency brake

Handle

Motor

Side handle

Bar

Chain

Cutting teeth

Starter cord

▲ Circular saws are used to cut logs into planks and wedges. A motor spins the saw's blade. Some circular saws have metre-wide blades which can cut whole tree trunks. The trunks pass along a moving track, called a conveyor belt, to the blade. The wood is cut straight as the trunk is moved along.

Electric clippers

A gardener uses an **electric** hedge clipper to cut a wide area of hedge in one sweep.

Electric hedge clippers have rows of sharp teeth set on two long blades. The blades lie on top of each other. As the teeth on the blades move apart twigs are trapped. When the teeth move together they act like tiny scissor blades to cut the twigs. ▼

A cut away view of how a garden hedge clipper works

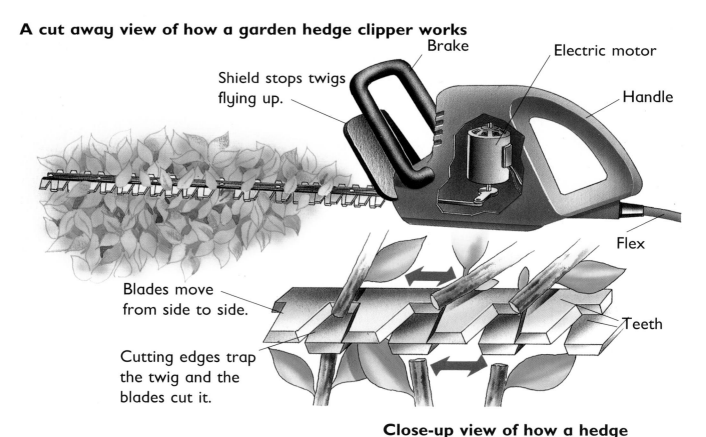

Brake

Electric motor

Shield stops twigs flying up.

Handle

Flex

Blades move from side to side.

Teeth

Cutting edges trap the twig and the blades cut it.

Close-up view of how a hedge clipper's blades cut twigs

◀ A motor moves the blades in opposite directions from side to side. This makes gaps open and close between the teeth. Twigs are first caught in the gaps then sliced as the blades cross.

Electricity is dangerous. Electric cutting tools should always be used with a **circuit breaker**, which will cut off the electricity in case the flex is cut accidentally.

Can openers

A simple can opener has a hooked blade which fits over the top of the can. When the handles are squeezed the blade punches a hole into the lid. ▼

Action of a simple can opener

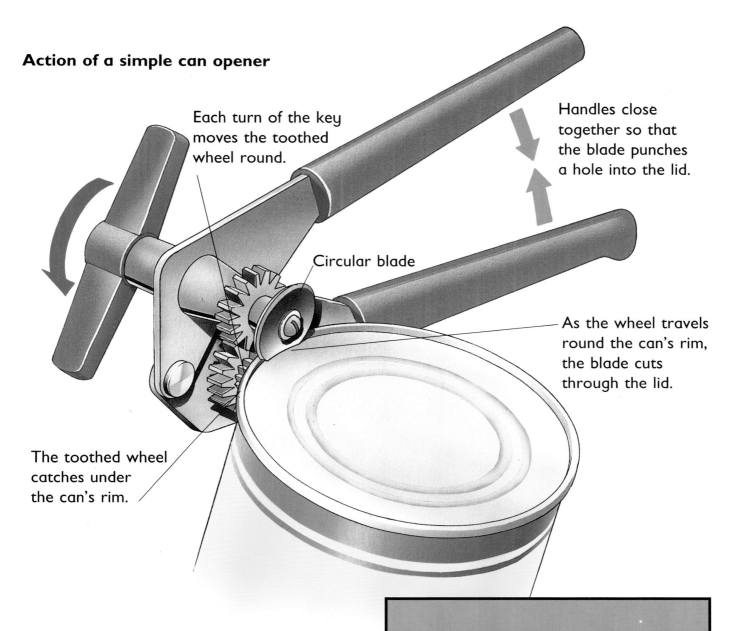

Each turn of the key moves the toothed wheel round.

Handles close together so that the blade punches a hole into the lid.

Circular blade

As the wheel travels round the can's rim, the blade cuts through the lid.

The toothed wheel catches under the can's rim.

▲ A toothed wheel grips the can's rim and a large key moves the wheel which turns the can. The circular blade cuts into the lid and removes it.

Warning! The cut edge of a lid is very sharp. Do not touch it.

Always wash can openers after use because dirt and old food may collect round the blade.

Augers

To cut holes in wood carpenters use an **auger**. Augers have a spiral of metal along their length with a sharp cutting blade at their end.

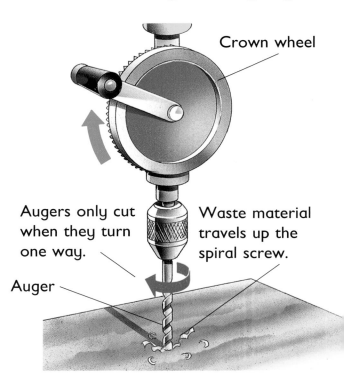

Crown wheel

Augers only cut when they turn one way.

Waste material travels up the spiral screw.

Auger

◀ Augers can be turned with a hand drill. The handle of the hand drill is turned round and round which gives more force to the cutting blade.

As the blade moves downwards the cut wood moves upwards and out of the spiral.

Cross-section of a construction auger

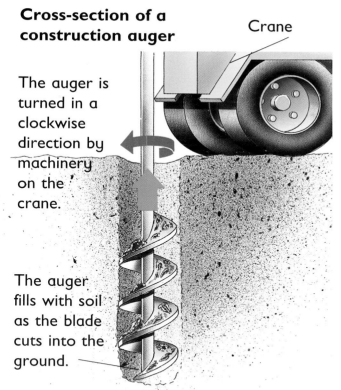

Crane

The auger is turned in a clockwise direction by machinery on the crane.

The auger fills with soil as the blade cuts into the ground.

◀ Huge construction augers cut deep holes in the ground for **piles** which are used for the foundations of buildings. Buildings need foundations to stop them sinking into the ground or falling down.

Machinery on a crane drives the auger. When the spiral section is filled with soil it is lifted out and emptied. ▼

Turning and lathes

Lathes allow us to cut lengths of wood or metal into round shapes. A pencil sharpener is a simple lathe. ▼

▲ The turning pencil is guided down a **funnel** to a fixed blade. Thin layers of wood and lead are removed. When the pencil's end fits into the funnel exactly, the blade stops cutting.

Working on a wood lathe is called 'turning'. Wood is held firmly in a stand. One end of the stand is made to spin, either by a foot pedal or an electric motor. The wood spins quickly and is cut by chisels or by blades fixed to the lathe itself. ▼

Spinning blades

When food is broken up into a pulp it is called a purée. Liquidizers chop fruit and vegetables into purées for desserts and soups.

Four sharp blades, fixed into the bottom of a jug, are spun by a motor. Liquid in the food is thrown outwards. The solid pieces sink to the bottom where the spinning blades can chop them. ▼

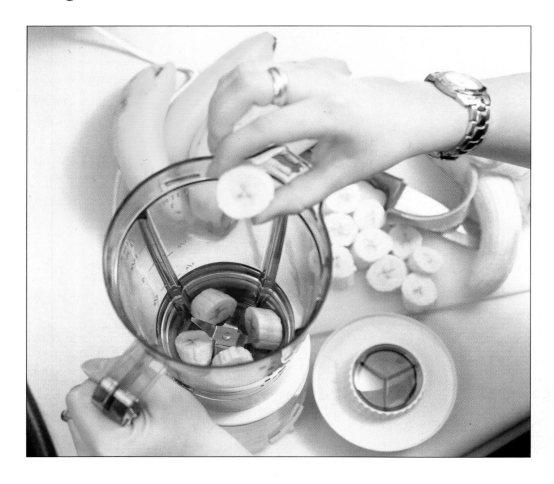

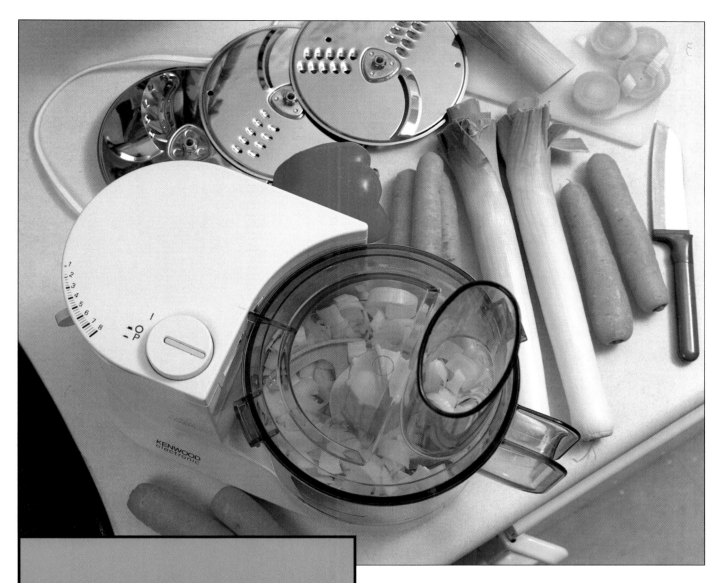

Warning! Spinning blades are very dangerous. Watch your fingers when emptying the food out of a liquidizer. Liquidizers and food processors only work when the lid is closed properly to stop people cutting themselves.

▲ Food processors are machines which can cut up and purée food. Processors have metal discs which have different shaped blades punched in them. These blades can grate, slice and even cut potatoes into chips.

Combine harvesters

To harvest, or cut and collect, a grain crop, such as wheat, in a big field farmers need to use large cutting machines, called combine harvesters. These huge machines do two jobs. They cut the long dry stalks of grain crops and separate out the grain. ▼

This diagram shows the inside workings of a combine harvester

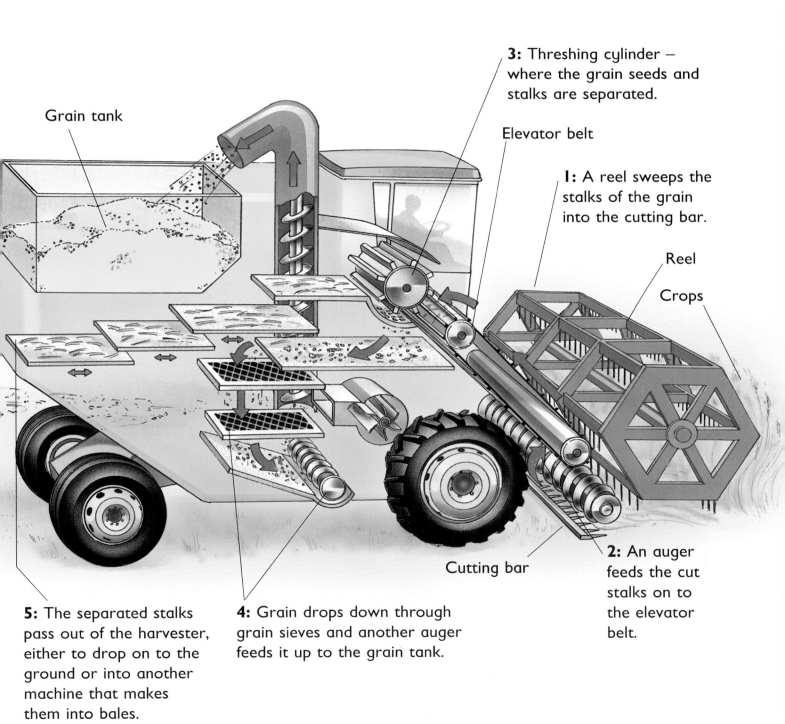

3: Threshing cylinder – where the grain seeds and stalks are separated.

Elevator belt

1: A reel sweeps the stalks of the grain into the cutting bar.

Grain tank

Reel

Crops

Cutting bar

2: An auger feeds the cut stalks on to the elevator belt.

5: The separated stalks pass out of the harvester, either to drop on to the ground or into another machine that makes them into bales.

4: Grain drops down through grain sieves and another auger feeds it up to the grain tank.

25

Cutting through rock

Fossil fuels, such as oil and coal, are found deep below the earth's surface. Special machines are used to cut through layers of rock to find these fuels.

Diamond is the hardest material known. It can cut materials which are too hard for steel blades. Diamond tipped drills are used on oil rigs to drill through rock for oil. ▼

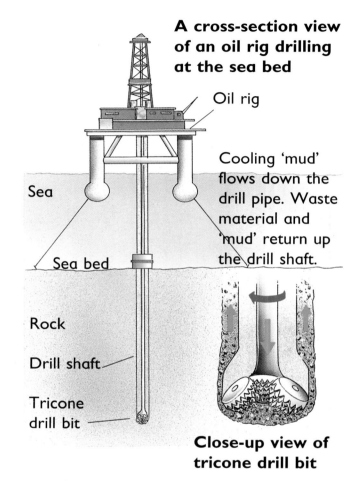

A cross-section view of an oil rig drilling at the sea bed

Oil rig

Cooling 'mud' flows down the drill pipe. Waste material and 'mud' return up the drill shaft.

Sea

Sea bed

Rock

Drill shaft

Tricone drill bit

Close-up view of tricone drill bit

▲ As the three heads of the diamond tipped drill turn, they grind through the rock.

The cutting tips of the drill get very hot. They are cooled by a special liquid, called 'mud', which is pumped down the drill pipe.

▲ This mining machine is used to cut coal as it is driven through a mine **shaft**. The top section has a belt with many sharp metal teeth. These cut the coal from the coal face as the belt goes round. The coal is scooped up by the bottom section of the machine.

Cutting without blades

Some cutting tools do not use blades.

Plastic wrapping film is most easily cut by a hot electric wire. Steel can be cut by heat from an **oxyacetylene torch.** ▼

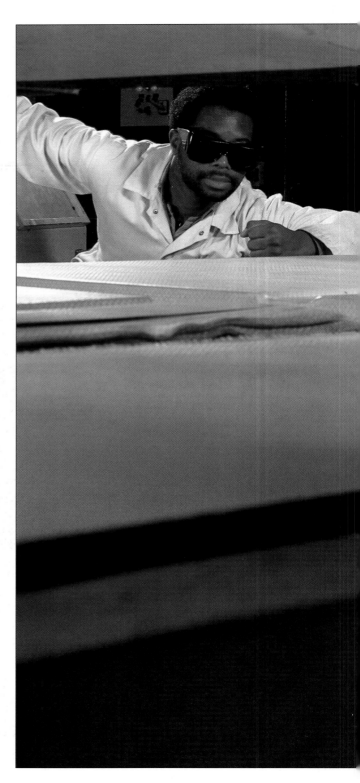

The most useful cutter without a blade is a laser. Lasers make a bright, narrow beam of light. This beam can cut through thick material or metal, such as blocks of steel. ▶

◀ Lasers can also be used for careful work, like shaping tiny parts for machines or cutting out shapes in thick plastic or foam.

Lasers are also used in hospitals. They are used to operate on delicate parts of the body, such as the eye. ▼

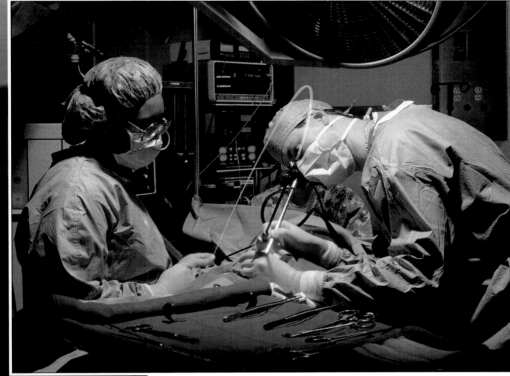

Glossary

auger A large screw which can be used to drill holes and carry away waste material.

bevel When a surface meets another at an angle. In cutting tools this means the blade cuts the surface of a material at an angle. The waste material curls away from the cutting edge.

circuit breaker A safety device which cuts off the electricity supply flowing through to an electric tool or machine.

electric Relating to electricity, which is a form of energy.

force The push or pull needed to move objects, or to change their speed or direction.

fossil fuels Sources of energy such as oil, gas and coal which are made from the bodies of dead animals and plants (fossils) which were left in the earth millions of years ago.

funnel A tube with a wide opening which narrows at the other end

levers Bars or rods which turn on a point called a pivot. A small effort over a large distance at one end of the rod produces a big force at the other end.

material Solid or loose matter, such as wood or earth.

mechanised When a tool is driven by a motor.

motor A machine which makes something work or move. A motor is worked by the energy from fuel, such as petrol, or by electricity.

oxyacetylene torch A tube which burns a mixture of gasses at high temperature. The heat can be directed on to a small area of a material, such as steel, for it to be cut.

piles Long blocks of steel or concrete which are driven deep into the ground as foundations for tall buildings.

pivot A point on which a lever turns freely.

shaft A deep hole or tunnel, such as the tunnels through a coal mine.

shavings The thin slices and chips of wood left after cutting.

Books to read

Cut it (Ways to... series) by H Pluckrose (Watts, 1993)

First Technology series by John Williams (Wayland, 1993)

Machines at Work (Science Discovery series) (Watts, 1993)

Starting Technology series by John Williams (Wayland, 1991)

Picture acknowledgements

Art Directors 5 (M. Peters); Aspect 19 (G. Thompkinson); British Coal 27; J. Allan Cash 9, 28; Cephas 7 (F. B. Higham), 11 (S. Boreham), *title page* and 12 (J. Marchington), 21 (P. A. Broadbent); C. M. Dixon 15; Eye Ubiquitous *cover inset* and 24 (P. Hutley), 26 (S. Lindridge); Tony Stone Worldwide 29; Reflections 8 (J. Woodcock), 28 – 9; Wayland Picture Library *cover background*, 4, 6, 16, 18, 20, 22, 23 (APM Studios, all); ZEFA 10, 13 (D. Baglin). All artwork is by Peter Bull.

Index